Contents

SECRETS OF
LOCK
PICKING

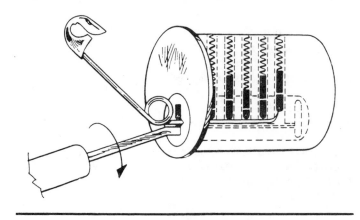

Steven Hampton

PALADIN PRESS
BOULDER, COLORADO

Also by Steven Hampton:

Advanced Lock Picking Secrets
Security Systems Simplified

Secrets of Lock Picking
by Steven Hampton

Copyright © 1987 by Steven Hampton

ISBN 0-87364-423-9
Printed in the United States of America

Published by Paladin Press, a division of
Paladin Enterprises, Inc., P.O. Box 1307,
Boulder, Colorado 80306, USA.
(303) 443-7250

Direct inquiries and/or orders to the above address.

Illustrations by Bill Border

Introduction

The ancient Egyptians were the first to come up with a complicated security device. This was the pin tumbler lock. We use the same security principle today on millions of applications.

The most commonly used lock today is the pin tumbler lock. A series of pins that are divided at certain points must be raised to these dividing points in relationship to the separation between the cylinder wall and the shell of the lock by a key cut for that particular series of pin divisions. Thus the cylinder can be turned, and the mechanism or lock is unlocked.

Lock picking means to open a lock by use of a flat piece of steel called a pick. Actually, the process requires two pieces of flat steel to open cylinder locks. It amuses me to watch spies and thieves on TV picking locks using only one tool. But it is for the better in a sense. If everyone learned how to pick locks by watching TV, we would all be at the mercy of anyone who wanted to steal from us, and the cylinder lock for the most part would be outdated.

The actual definition of lock picking should be: "The manipulation and opening of any restrictive mechanical or electronic device by usage of tools other than the implied instrument (key or code) used solely for that device." A little lengthy, but more accurate description. With cylinder locks, it requires a *pick* and a *tension wrench*.

By picking the lock, you simply replace the function of a key with a pick that raises the pins to their "breaking point," and using a tension wrench one rotates the cylinder to operate the cam at the rear of the lock's cylinder to unlock the mechanism.

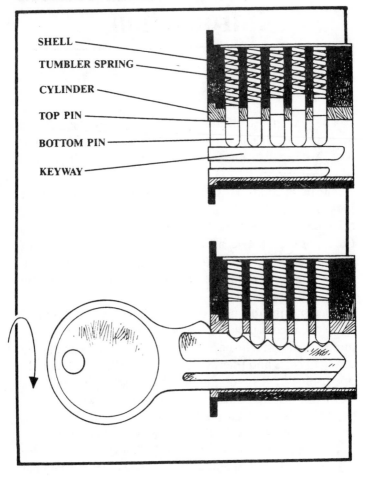

SHELL

TUMBLER SPRING

CYLINDER

TOP PIN

BOTTOM PIN

KEYWAY

Figure 1. The pin tumbler lock, cutaway view.

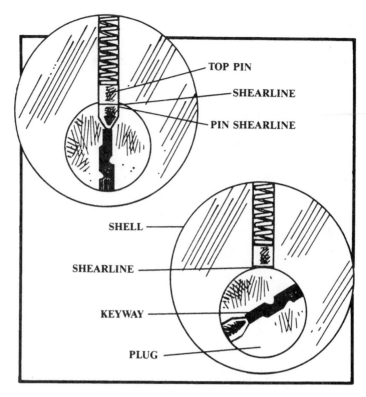

Figure 2. The pin tumbler lock, front view.

The tension wrench is used to apply tension to the cylinder of the lock to cause a slight binding action on the pins as well as to turn the cylinder after the pins have been aligned by the pick; this opens the lock. The slight binding action on the pins caused by the tension wrench allows one to hear and feel each pin as it "breaks" or reaches alignment with the separation of cylinder and shell. The vibration is felt in the knuckles and joints of the fingers, and the sound is similar to that of a cricket in an arm wrestling match—a subtle yet distinct click.

Usually you need very little tension with the wrench while picking the lock. In fact, it takes somewhat of a delicate, yet firm touch. This is the secret to picking locks successfully—a firm and yet gentle touch on the tension wrench. You should be able to feel the pins click into place with the right amount of tension; experience will be your true guide.

Half of your success will be based on your ability to use or improvise various objects to use as tools for your purpose. The other half will depend on practice. I once picked a pin tumbler lock using a borrowed roach clip and a hairpin. A dangerous fire was prevented and probably several lives were saved. The world is full of useful objects for the purpose, so never hesitate to experiment.

Tools

I started picking locks using a small screwdriver and a safety pin. The screwdriver can be used as a tension wrench, and the safety pin is used like a "hook" pick. The last half inch of the screwdriver's tip was bent at a 45 degree angle so as to allow easy entry for the pick (bent safety pin). Do not heat the screwdriver tip to bend it, as this will destroy its temper. Use a vise and hammer to do the job. Bend slowly by using firm and short taps of the hammer, otherwise you may break and weaken the shaft. The safety pin should be about one and a half inches long and bent in the same way.

With the small screwdriver as a tension wrench, you can use more of a turning or twisting movement than with a regular tension wrench so you will generally need less direct force when using it. As I mentioned earlier, with practice you will develop the feeling for the right amount of tension on a cylinder. If the safety pin bends after a short time, use the keyway of the lock you are picking to bend it back into shape. Even after several times of bending, it should still be useful. Keep a few spares handy, though. File the tip of the safety pin flat in relationship to the bottom of the pins in the lock. Smooth any sharp edges so that you won't impale yourself. Also, if the tip is smooth, the pick will not get hung up on the pins while picking the lock.

Granted these are not the best tools for the job, but they do work. If you learn to use your junk box as a rich source of equipment, then with your experience real lock picks will give you magic fingers. Also, you'll have the advantage of being able to improvise should you be without the real things (which are illegal to carry on your person in most parts of the country).

Lock picks are difficult to get. I received my first set when I became a locksmith apprentice. All of my subsequent sets I made from stainless steel steak knives with a grinder and cut-off wheel. They are much more durable than the commercial picks. If you do make your own, make certain that the steel is quenched after every 3 seconds of grinding—do not allow the pick to get hot to the point of blue discoloration.

A diamond pick is the standard pick I use on most all pin and wafer locks. A small diamond pick is used for small pin tumbler locks such as small Master padlocks, cabinet file locks, etc. The tubular cylinder lock pick, we will discuss later. The double-ended, single-pronged tension wrench is used with the diamond pick. It features double usage; a small end for small cylinders and a large end for the larger cylinders. A special tension wrench is used for double-wafer cylinder locks with an end with two prongs on one end and tubular cylinder locks with the single prong on the other end. We will discuss tubular cylinder and double-wafer locks later as well. The steel should be .030 inches to .035 inches thick for the picks and .045 inches to .050 inches thick for the first tension wrench mentioned above. The second tension wrench should be .062 inches square (.062 inches × .062 inches) on the tubular cylinder side (one pronged end), and .045 inches thick on the double-wafer end (two-pronged end). You can accomplish this by starting out with .045 inches in thickness. The two-pronged end should be bent carefully in a vise at a 30 degree angle. This allows easy entry for the pick on double-wafer locks.

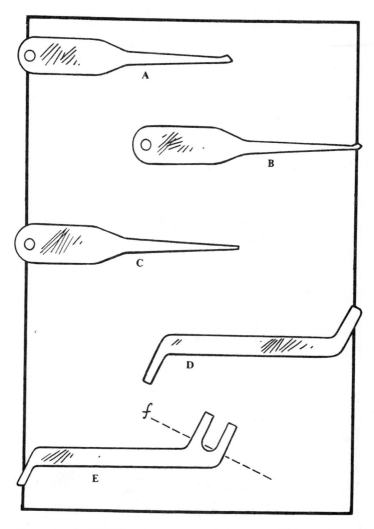

Figure 3. A: a diamond pick; B: a small diamond pick; C: a tubular cylinder lock pick; D: a tension wrench, used with the diamond picks; E: a tension wrench intended for double-wafer cylinder locks and tubular cylinder locks.

Among the more common tools used by professionals around the world is the *rake* pick. The rake pick is used to "rake" the tumblers into place by sliding it in and out across the tumblers. I seldom use the rake pick because it is not highly effective and I consider it a sloppy excuse for a lock pick. I've seen the rake pick work on some difficult locks, but you can rake with a diamond pick and get the same results. I prefer the diamond pick for most tumbler locks simply because it is easier to get in and out of locks—it slides across the tumblers with little or no trouble.

A ball pick is used for picking double-wafer cylinder locks, though I never carry one; I use a large diamond pick and reverse it when picking these locks. This means I have one less pick to carry and lose.

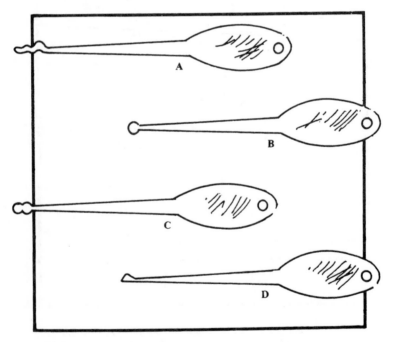

Figure 4. A: a rake pick; B: a ball pick; C: a double ball pick; D: a diamond pick.

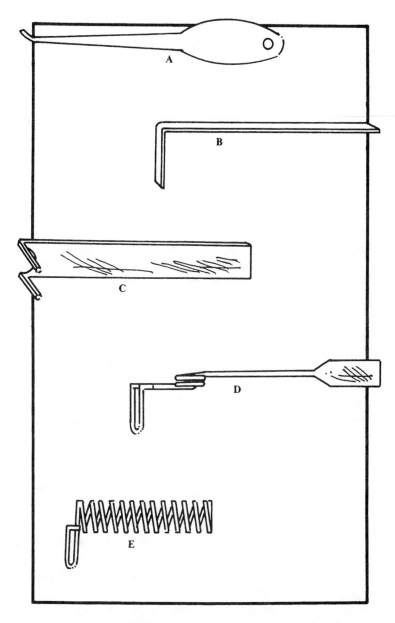

Figure 5. A: a hook pick; B: a pin and wafer lock tension wrench; C: a double-wafer tension wrench; D: a Feather Touch tension wrench; E: a homemade Feather Touch tension wrench.

A double-ball pick is used like a rake on double-wafer locks in conjunction with a tension wrench (two-pronged end).

A hook pick is used to open lever tumbler locks, though again, I use a diamond pick with a hooking action when possible. There are various sizes of hooks but they all have the same basic job—to catch the movable levers that unlock lever locks.

There are also various sizes of tension wrenches. They are usually made from spring steel. The standard tension wrench is used for pin and wafer locks. A special tension wrench is called a *Feather Touch*, and it is used for high-security mushroom and spool pin tumbler locks. Its delicate spring-loaded action allows the pick to bypass the tendencies of these pins to stick. A homemade version of the Feather Touch can be made from a medium-light duty steel spring.

As to getting lock picks for your own use, you cannot go down to your local hardware store and buy them. I could supply you with some sources or wholesalers, but I do believe it is illegal for them to sell to individuals. Your best bet would be to find a machine shop that will fabricate them for you. It would be less expensive and arouse less suspicion if you purchase a small grinder with a cut-off wheel and make your own. With a little practice, you can make a whole set in an afternoon. Use a copy of the illustrations in this book as templates and carefully cut them out with an X-ACTO knife. Cut down the middle of the lines. Acquire some stainless steel (many steak knives approach proper thickness).

With a glue stick, lightly coat one side of the paper template and apply it to the cleaned stainless surface, and allow it to dry. You'll need a can of black wrinkle finish spray paint. This kind of paint has a high carbon content and can stand high temperature of grinding. Spray the stainless (or knives) with the patterns glued on and dry in a warm oven or direct sunlight for one hour. Set aside for twenty-four more hours. Peel off the paper template and you are ready to cut and grind. Please use caution when cutting and grinding. The piece should be quenched every three seconds in cold water. Smooth up sharp edges with a small file or burnishing wheel.

Tools made from stainless steel will outlast the purchased ones. The tools purchased from most suppliers are made from spring steel and wear out after about 100 uses. The stainless steel ones, if properly made, should last over 2,000 uses.

Lock Identification

There are many types of locks, the most common being:

1. *The pin tumbler lock.* Used for house and garage doors, padlocks, mail boxes, and Ford automobiles.
2. *The wafer tumbler lock.* Used for garage and trailer doors, desks, padlocks, cabinets, most autos, window locks, and older vending machines.
3. *The double-wafer lock.* Used for higher security wafer tumbler applications.
4. *The warded locks.* Used for light security padlocks and old-fashioned door locks.
5. *Lever locks.* Used for light security and older padlocks, sophisticated safe-deposit boxes, some desks, jewelry boxes, and small cash boxes.
6. *Tubular cylinder locks.* Used for alarm control systems, newer vending machines, car-wash control boxes and wherever higher security problems might exist.

These locks are the more common locks used yet there are variations and combinations of these principal types that usually pick open in the manner that will be discussed. Some of them just require practice of the basic types, others luck, and most of the rest of them knowledge of how that particular lock works and is keyed. This comes from experience.

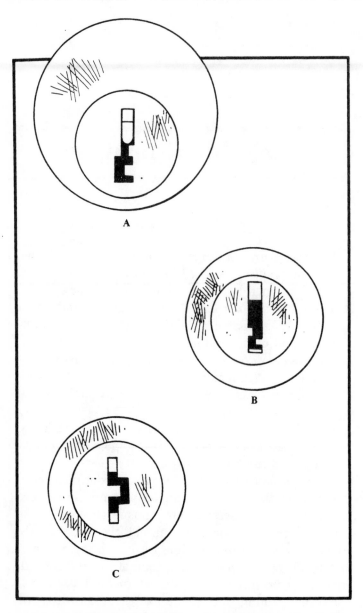

Figure 6. A: a pin tumbler lock; B: a wafer tumbler lock; C: a double-wafer tumbler lock.

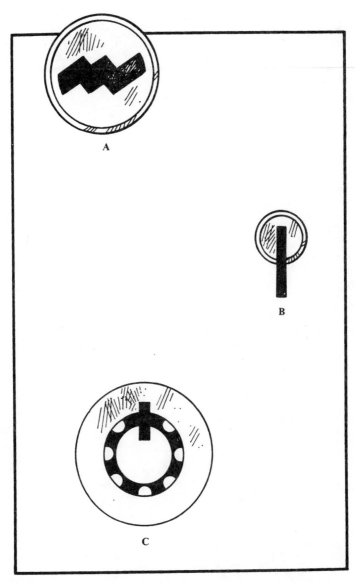

Figure 7. A: a warded lock; B: a lever lock; C: a tubular cylinder lock.

Pin Tumbler Locks

Pin tumbler locks offer the most security for their price. They have close machine tolerances and approximately 1,000,000 different key combinations for a five-pin lock. Considering the thousands of different companies making pin tumblers (different shaped keyways for each company or design line), the chances of someone having a key that will work in your front door lock are one in many billions.

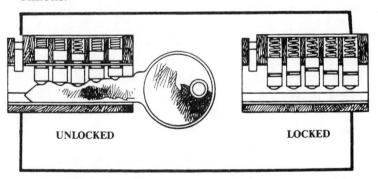

UNLOCKED   LOCKED

Figure 8. A pin tumbler lock.

Pin tumbler locks can easily be identified by peering down the keyway and locating the first round pin.

Sometimes you can see the pin's dividing point, where it breaks with the cylinder wall (shear point).

To successfully pick a pin tumbler lock, your sense of touch sould be honed so that both hands feel the tools. Once the hand holding the pick has located a slight relief in tension while picking a particular tumbler, the other hand holding the tension wrench will feel a relief or breaking point. Both hands should be involved with the sense of touch, the sensing of the inner workings of the lock.

We are now ready to begin the first lesson. First open your front door and check for a pin tumbler lock on it. It should have one on it. If there is one, leave the door open to decrease suspicion. Do not lock yourself out of your apartment or house by being overconfident; not only will you raise suspicion, but window glass is not cheap.

HOW TO PICK A TUMBLER LOCK

STEP ONE

Without using the tension wrench, slip the pick into the lock. The "hook" of the pick should be toward the tumblers (up in most cases, depending on whether or not the lock was mounted upside down—you can tell by looking down the keyway and locating the first pin with your pick). Try to feel the last tumbler of the lock. It should be 7/8 inches into the lock for a five-pin tumbler lock (most common pin tumbler lock used).

Make certain that you have no tension on the wrench when inserting the pick as this will encumber the frontal tumblers. When you feel the back tumbler, slowly raise it with a *slight* prying motion of the pick. Release it, but keep the pick in the lock on the rear tumbler.

Now insert the tension wrench, allowing room for the pick to manipulate all of the pins. It should be placed at the bottom of the cylinder if the lock was mounted upright, tumblers toward the top of the cylinder. Apply firm and yet gentle clockwise pressure to the tension wrench.

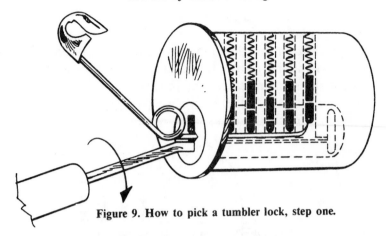

Figure 9. How to pick a tumbler lock, step one.

Slowly raise the back tumbler with a slight prying motion of the pick. A minute click will be felt and heard when it breaks. It will lose its springiness when this occurs, so do not go any further with it. Any further movement with the pick will cause binding by going past the pins' shear line. Continue an even pressure with the tension wrench.

Keeping an even tension pressure, proceed to Step Two.

STEP TWO

The fourth tumbler should be easily felt since it is the next one in line. Raise it until it breaks, keeping the tension wrench steady. It too will give a sound and sensation when it breaks or aligns.

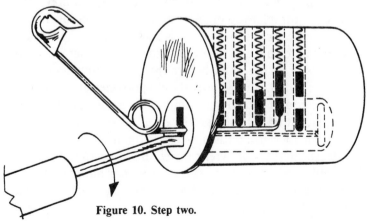

Figure 10. Step two.

STEP THREE

The third or middle tumbler is next. Again, it too will click. Maintain a constant, even pressure on the wrench—about the same pressure that you would use to replace a cap on a catsup bottle. You may feel the "clicks" in your tension wrench as well as hear them.

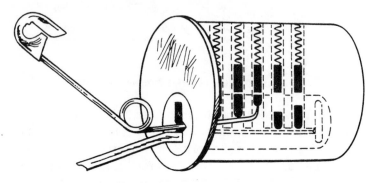

Figure 11. Step three.

STEPS FOUR AND FIVE

Continue on to the next tumbler out, working toward you. When it breaks, raise the last (front) tumbler to its braking point and the cylinder should be free to rotate and unlock the door. Sometimes you may have to play with the wrench to open the lock because you may have raised a tumbler too high, past its breaking point. If this is the case, *very* slowly and gradually release the tension wrench pressure and the overly extended tumbler will drop into its breaking point before the other tumblers have a chance to fall. The cylinder should pop open at that point. I have found that this technique is responsible for over 30 percent of my successes in opening all tumbler locks.

If the lock still refuses to open after all that treatment, release the tension wrench pressure, allowing all of the tumblers to drop and start over. You may have more than one tumbler too high and would be better off to repeat the picking process.

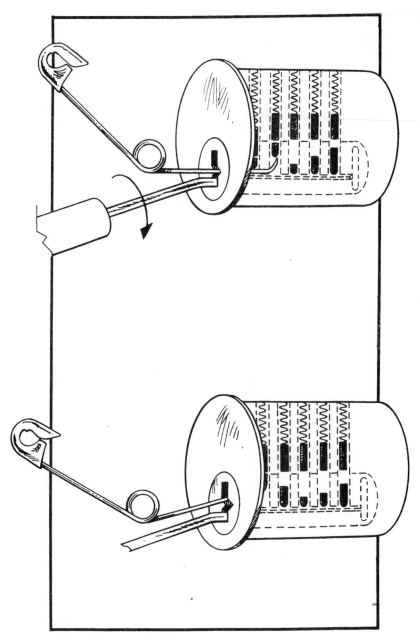

Figure 12. Step four (top), and step five (above).

Wafer Tumbler Locks

Wafer tumbler locks make up over one-fourth of the locks in use in the world. Since they are generally easier to pick than most pin tumbler locks, you will be 75 percent master after fooling around with these mechanisms. That is why I wrote about pin tumbler locks first—they are more difficult and make up over one-half of the locks used today.

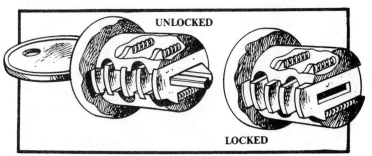

Figure 13. A wafer tumbler lock.

The term *wafer* refers to the general shape of the tumblers. The wafers are flat, spring-loaded tumblers that are much thinner than pins and the distance between them is less. Wafer locks are picked in the same way as pin tumbler locks, but you must compensate for the smaller dimensions. You can identify wafer locks simply by looking down the keyway and locating the first flat tumbler. The last tumbler on most wafer locks is located about one-half inch into the lock.

Wafer locks are used on filing cabinets, lockers, most cars, garage doors, desks, and wherever medium security is required. The only wafer tumbler lock in common use that is difficult to pick is the side-bar wafer lock. It is the most popular type of auto lock. This lock is of different design than most other locks and offers much more security than a regular wafer tumbler lock, or even a pin tumbler lock.

The side bar lock is used mostly on General Motors cars and trucks since 1935. It is used on ignitions, door, and trunk locks. Side bar locks are hard to pick because you cannot feel or hear the tumblers align with the cylinders breaking point. A spring-loaded bar falls into place to allow the cylinder to turn when all of the tumblers are aligned. There is no way to tell when that happens. One learns to sense the bar while picking so that it seems to fall into place by itself. But for beginners, I recommend this technique for emergency openings: Peer down the keyway and locate the side groove of any of the tumblers using a pick as a searching tool. Drill a small hole in the shell of the lock above the bar which is above the grooves on the tumblers. Since side bar locks have off-centered keyways, the usual place to drill is opposite of the keyway. Using an L-shaped steel wire, put pressure on the sidebar and rake the tumblers using a tension wrench for cylinder rotation and the lock will open.

Fortunately, most GMC autos have inferior window seals; with a coat hanger, one can lasso the locking door knob to open the door. If you are going to be successful at opening side bars, you will do it within two minutes; otherwise, you are causing unnecessary wear on your picks not to mention wasting your time.

Ford auto locks are relatively simple to pick. They have

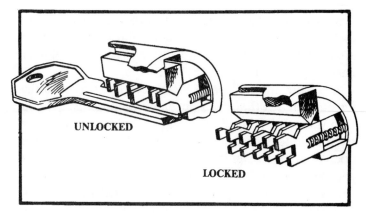

Figure 14. A side bar lock.

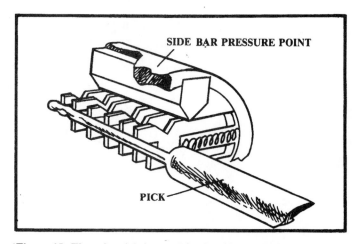

Figure 15. The rake pick inserted in the side bar lock.

pin tumblers and you have to remember that the door locks turn counterclockwise. Most other auto locks turn clockwise. If you are not sure, remember this: If the tumblers will not catch at their breaking points, you are going in the wrong direction with the tension wrench.

Wafer locks are a cinch to pick if you have learned how to pick pin tumblers. Just remember that wafers are thinner than pins and there is less distance between them.

Generally you need less tension-wrench pressure with these locks, yet car locks can be quite stubborn and require a great deal of tension. Any heavily spring-loaded cylinder needs a substantial amount of tension.

As a rule, though, wafer locks need less play with the tension wrench than with pin tumbler locks. But if you find yourself having difficulty in opening these, you may try a little tension-wrench play. Usually they won't pop open like pin tumbler locks, they just slide open; you don't get the warning that a pin tumbler gives before it opens because there is less contact area on the wafer's edge than on a pin, so the sense of climax is reduced with these types of locks. Still, they open quite easily.

Double Wafer Locks

Double-wafer locks are picked in the same way as single-wafer locks, but there are two sides to the story. Not only do you have to align the top wafers, but you have ones in the bottom of the cylinder to align as well.

The Chicago Lock Company was the first to come up with this type of lock. It is a classic example of the race toward better security. Certain tension wrenches allow uninterrupted picking using ball picks. You can also use a standard tension wrench or small screwdriver and place it at the center of the keyway. To eliminate unnecessary baggage, use a diamond pick, reversing it to encounter both top and bottom wafers.

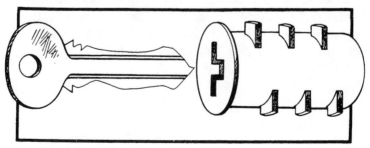

Figure 16. A double-wafer lock.

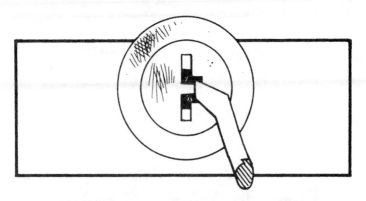

Figure 17. Inserting a tension wrench in a double-wafer lock.

The last tumbler in this type of lock is located less than one-half of an inch in. The picking procedure may have to be repeated more than one time—top wafers, then bottom wafers, top, bottom—back and forth. Yet these locks are easier to pick than most pin tumblers.

Locate the last wafer on the top side and move it to its breaking point. Do the same with the other top wafers. Keep the tension wrench firm, remove the pick, turn it upside down (if you are using a diamond or homemade pick), and reinsert it to work the bottom wafers. You may have to repeat this process a few times, but double-wafer locks can and will open with such treatment. Schlage has a doorknob lock that opens this way, but the last tumbler is about one and one-half inches in.

Double-wafer locks are easy to master if you have learned to pick pin and wafer tumbler locks. Since double-wafer locks are more compact, you have to compensate for the fact—slightly closer tolerances. These type of locks are used on old pop and candy machines, gas caps, cabinets, etc.

Pin and Wafer Tumbler Padlocks

Cylinder padlocks require a technique of holding them with the same hand with which you are using the tension wrench. This technique allows one to pick the padlock without going into contortions over a dangling padlock. Assuming that you are right-handed, hold the padlock in your left hand by gripping the body of the padlock with your thumb and forefinger. Insert the tension wrench at the bottom of the keyway and hold it in a clockwise turn with your ring and little finger, causing a slight binding pressure on the cylinder. Now your right hand is free to pick, and your left hand does the job of holding both the lock and tension wrench. The overhand method works well, too, but the thumb controls the tension wrench instead. Switch around to find which is most comfortable for you.

When tumbler padlocks pop open, it is quite a sensation because the shackle is spring-loaded and gives one quite a jolt. It's a feeling of accomplishment. You may need a little more tension on padlocks than on door locks because the cylinder cam has to operate a spring-loaded bolt. Overall, padlocks are the most fun to open. Practice using old or discarded padlocks that you have found. I've worn out hundreds of them.

Warded and Lever Locks

Now that you have become proficient at picking pin and wafer tumbler locks, let's proceed to simpler mechanisms, the warded and lever locks.

A warded lock is one that allows a key to act upon an unlocking cam by passing various restrictions known as wards. Actually, they are quite simple locks—one of the first used in American history.

With warded padlocks, the key turns either right or left to spread the locking spring. The locking spring is the only thing that holds the shackle in a locked position. The key to open this lock has to be turned one-quarter turn. As the locking spring is separated, the shackle opens.

All warded padlocks are basically the same, with slight variations existing by individual manufacturers. It would be impossible to show all of the various warded padlocks in this book, but they all work the same.

The laminated warded padlock is very popular now and one of the most expensive. It offers more security than most of the others and has a hardened-steel shackle.

Warded padlocks are very simple to pick. They require that you have the sense of touch you developed from picking pin and wafer locks. You have to feel the locking

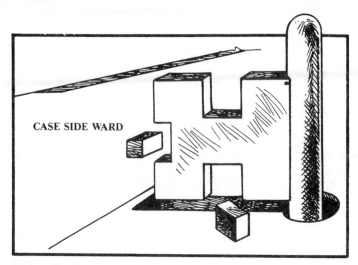

Figure 18. A warded lock.

springs and learn to bypass the wards, or stationary chambers of the lock. A homemade T-shaped pick for warded padlocks and an L-shaped pick for most lever locks are easy to make. They are made from 1/32 inch steel piano wire. I have successfully used homemade L-shaped tools on warded padlocks, but it is a little more difficult than the T-shaped tools.

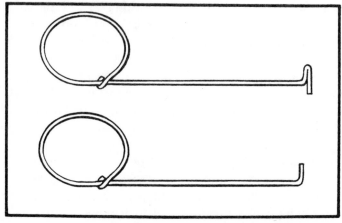

Figure 19. The T-shaped pick (top), and the L-shaped pick (above).

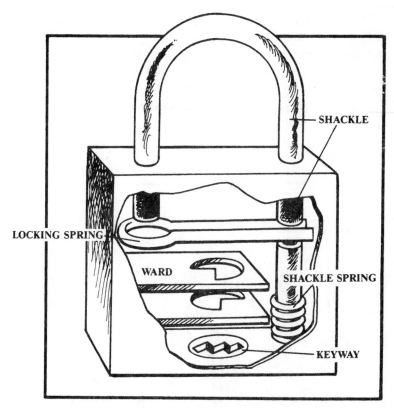

Figure 20. One cutaway view of a warded padlock.

By using a twisting action with the pick key, you can feel whether or not you have located the actuating spring or a stationary ward. When you have located the locking springs, gently twist the pick key to open it. Push in on the shackle while doing this and release to hold each spring if it is a two-spring warded padlock. Working back and forth in this manner will open the padlock.

Most warded padlocks have only one locking spring. They are small, and they are the ones you should start with. The bigger ones do have two springs, and you should work one spring at a time while slightly working the shackle in and out until it pops open.

In most cases, it is easier to make your own pick keys. They should be .050 inches thick.

A warded padlock can be opened by any one of the Five Magic Keys shown below. These five pick keys can open over 200 different types of warded padlocks used today. The pick key is used for lever padlocks and in some cases for a few warded ones.

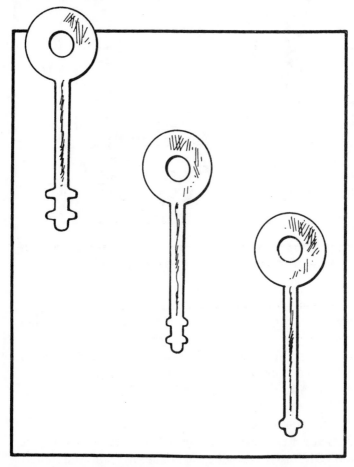

Figure 21. Of the Five Magic Keys, above left is the large double spring warded key, the small double spring warded key (middle), and at the right the small single spring warded key.

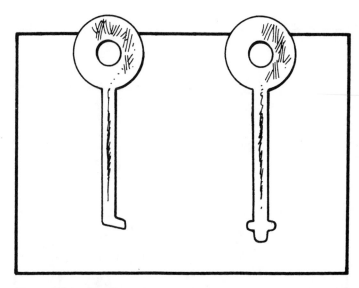

Figure 22. Of the Five Magic Keys, the lever lock key is on the left, and the large single spring warded key is on the right.

Lever locks are slightly more complex than warded locks. You have to catch the right levers to activate the bolt or shackle spring to unlock the lock. Again, feel has a major role in opening these locks—you have to search for the spring-loaded levers and rotate them 45 degrees in the direction of the lever location; in other words, turn towards the side on which the levers are located.

For desk-type lever-locks, there are two parts that have to be moved to open or close them—the lever and the bolt. If you were to put pressure against the bolt and push it in, you will notice that the "stop" will not allow it to go in since it hits the levers.

If the levers are raised to their respective heights, the bolt can be operated to open the lock by motion of the key. When the proper key is inserted in the lock, the notches in the key are cut so that they line up all the levers and allow the stop to enter the gates. At the same time, the key forces the bolt in or out.

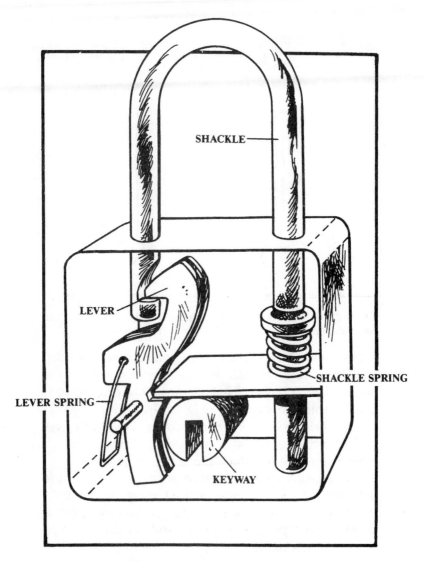

Figure 23. A simple lever padlock.

In order to pick the lever-lock, you are going to have to line up the levers and draw the bolt back to the open position. Remember, if this lock is still in the desk, you

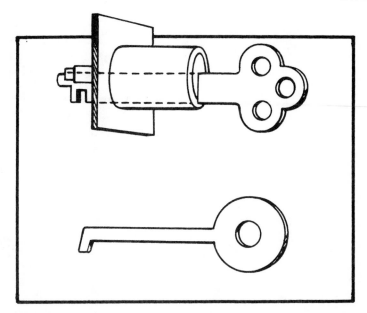

Figure 24. At the top is a lever key in its keyhole guide. Use the lever-lock Magic Key (above) to pick the lever-lock.

will not be able to see any of the moving parts unless you use a penlight. By rotating the keyhold guide while shining your light in the keyway, you will be able to locate the levers.

Using the L-shaped lever pick, you can push back the levers and catch the bolt using a turning motion in a searching fashion. This will take some practice but once you have opened it, it will become easier each successive time. Practice with an unmounted lock.

Tubular Cylinder Locks

We will gradually proceed to more sophisticated locks from here. I would like to remind you that success is not based on personality. If one is arrogant about one's lock-picking skills, one could easily be made a fool of by a lock. And no matter how many times you bash a cylinder, you will still be locked out. The only thing you accomplish is attracting an audience—so be cool.

If at this point you have had much difficulty understanding the principles of pin and wafer locks, please restudy this book from the beginning. Read it several times so as to absorb it. The information that you now have has taken me almost two decades to gather, so please be mindful of that.

Now you are about to learn how to open the more difficult locking mechanisms—some of the other 25 percent of the locks used today. You should feel confident with pin, wafer and double-wafer tumbler locks before you attempt rim cylinder locks.

Tubular cylinder locks stand out as the most generally accepted lock in all important industries using high-quality locks for protection of property, merchandise, and cash. They are recognized as giving the maximum amount of

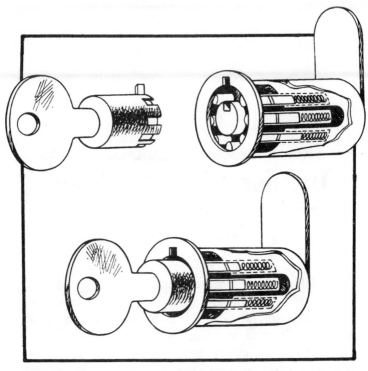

Figure 25. The tubular cylinder lock locked (top), and unlocked (above).

security for their price range.

Tubular cylinder locks are pin tumbler locks arranged on a circular plane. Unlike conventional pin tumbler locks, all of the pins are exposed to the eye. The central section of the lock rotates to operate the cam when all of the seven pins have reached their breaking points. When the proper key is entered into the lock, the tumblers are pressed into position so that the central section (plug) can be turned. This manual operation of inserting the key places the tumblers in position so that the lock can be operated and ensures that frost, dust, salt, or unfavorable climatic conditions will not affect the smooth operation of the lock.

The Chicago Ace lock is a product of the Chicago Lock

Company of Chicago, Illinois. It is an effective security device and is used on vending machines, coin boxes, and burglar alarms. A larger, more complex version of it is used on bank doors and electronic teller machines. The key is of tubular shape with the cuts arranged in a circle around the key.

The pick used for this lock is the tubular cylinder pick, or you may use a straight pin or your homemade safety pin pick. The one-pronged end of the tension wrench is a little more specialized and is used for rim cylinder locks. It must be .062 inches square for best results. Any square steel stock is acceptable, as long as it fits snugly into the groove of the tubular cylinder plug.

This type of lock is a burglar's nightmare because it takes so long to pick. You have to pick it three or four times to accomplish the unlocking radius of 120 to 180 degrees. And the cylinder locks after each time you pick it—every one-seventh of a turn.

If you leave the lock only partly picked, the key will not be able to open it, so you must pick it back into the locked position after opening it—another three or four picking sessions. In all, to unlock and lock the cylinder, you have to pick it up to eight times—quite a chore if you don't have the right tools or time.

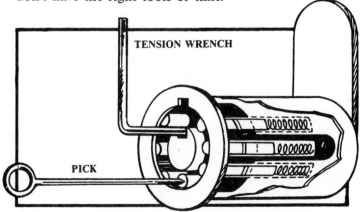

Figure 26. Picking a tubular cylinder lock.

These locks almost always pick in the clockwise direction. Make certain that the tension wrench fits snugly into the groove on the cylinder. Very slowly push the first pin down until it clicks, maintaining a definite clockwise pressure on the tension wrench. Once the tumbler has broken, do not push any further and proceed to the next one, and so on. As you reach the last tumbler, the tension wrench will feel more slack and give way if the lock were properly picked.

There are special keyhole saws for these locks in which you drill out the tumblers and turn the cylinder. Also, there is a special tool used by locksmiths to open rim cylinder locks.

Mushroom and Spool Pin Tumbler Locks

High-security pin tumbler locks may contain specially made pins to make picking them more challenging. The pins are machined so as to make picking them quite difficult. When picking these locks, the pins give the impression that they have broken, when in fact they could be a long way from breaking. You can tell whether or not you are picking a pin tumbler lock that has these pins by the fact that the pins seem to align so easily with a louder than normal click. The cylinder seems eager to open but to no avail.

Figure 27. The spool pin is at left, and the mushroom pin is at right.

The picking procedure relies on a well-yielding tension wrench. The tension wrench has to be lightly spring-loaded so that the pins can bypass their false breaking points. You also have to "rake" (seesaw in and out) the pins with your pick. The feather-touch tension wrench is ideal for the job. Use light pressure with it, and it will let you in.

The mushroom and spool pins are used in locks for high-security purposes such as bank doors. The American Lock Company uses them in some of their padlocks.

Magnetic Locks

Magnetic locks are fascinating. I almost hate to open them because I feel that I have breached their uniqueness. In reality, you do not pick them, but "confuse" them. They generally work on the principle that like magnetic polarities repel each other. The key is a set of small magnets arranged in a certain order to repel other magnets in the lock, thereby allowing the spring-loaded bolt or cam to open the lock.

By using a pulsating electromagnetic field, you can cause the magnets in the lock to vibrate violently at thirty vibrations per second, thereby allowing it to be opened

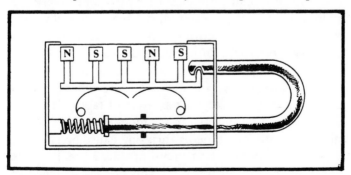

Figure 28. The inner mechanism of a magnetic lock is rather simple.

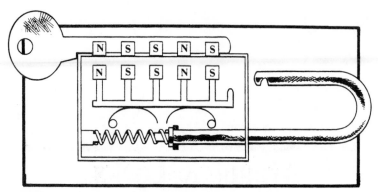

Figure 29. The magnetic key has the same sequence of magnets as the lock.

by intermittent tugging of the bolt or turning of the door knob.

This method may also ruin the small magnets in the lock by changing their magnetic status or properties. So, if you have to perform an emergency break-in with these locks, do not relock the door. The card or key will not operate the lock.

The magnetic pick can be used on padlocks by stroking it across the place where the key is placed. It is also designed to fit into the doorknob and is used by stroking one pole in and out or by using the other pole the same way.

If you have had little or no training and experience building something like this, please have a friend who is familiar with basic electronics do it for you. Do not take the chance of electrocuting yourself. Make sure that the coil is also completely covered with electrician's tape after you have wound the 34 gauge wire. Also make sure that the steel core has at least three layers of tape over it. Do not leave the unit plugged in for more than two to three minutes at any one time as this may cause overheating which could cause it to burn out or start a fire. It *is* safe to use if constructed properly and not left plugged in unattended. Opening magnetic locks requires only 30 to 60 seconds anyway, so don't leave the unit plugged in for longer.

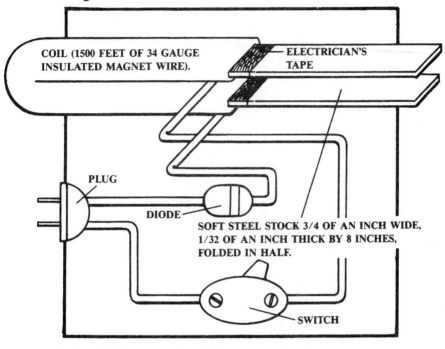

Figure 30. The magnetic pick is easy to construct.

For magnetic padlocks, use a back-and-forth stroking action along the length of the keyway. For magnetic door locks, use a stroking in-and-out action in the slot of the knob alternating from one side (pole) of the pick to the other.

The "key" for a magnetic door lock is a metal or plastic card containing an array of magnetic domains or regions coded in a specific order to allow entry. The magnetic pick bypasses that.

Disk Tumbler Locks

Combination or "puzzle" locks were invented to further improve security and the protection of valuables. The older safes and lockboxes were good security devices when they came into the market, but some people became curious and realized that these safe locks had inherent weaknesses. One of the main problems was that the disk tumblers were not mechanically isolated from the bolt that unlocks the safe door. In other words, you could feel and hear the tumblers while turning the dial by applying pressure on the handle of the bolt.

When that problem was recognized and solved, thieves started drilling through strategic places in the lock itself to open it. Knocking off hinges was an all-time favorite tactic as well. Then came punching out the dial shaft, blowtorching, and just plain blowing the door with explosives. Greed can breed great creativity.

The first problem, that of manipulating the tumblers open, was rectified by making use of the dial to operate the bolt upon completion of the dialing of the correct combination. This made it nearly impossible to feel or hear the tumblers. Drilling was deterred by laminating the safe

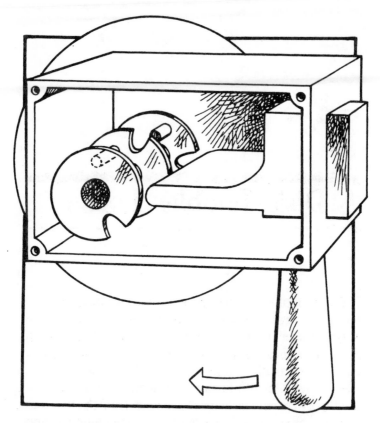

Figure 31. A disk tumbler safe lock.

door with hard steel and beryllium-copper plates. The beryllium-copper plates pull heat away from the drill tip quickly, and the bit just spins without effect; drilling cannot take place without the generation of heat at the bit's cutting edges. Knocking off hinges was discouraged by using three or more bolts operated by a main linkage network. Punching out the dial shaft to let the tumblers fall out of the way of the bolt was corrected by beveling the shaft into the wall of the safe door.

Presently, safe locks are quite sophisticated. Picking them would require supernatural power. The older safes, however, are much easier and even fun to pick. Picking combination padlocks is a good way to start learning how to open safes, and we will get to them shortly. But first, let us discuss some basic principles of disk tumbler locks.

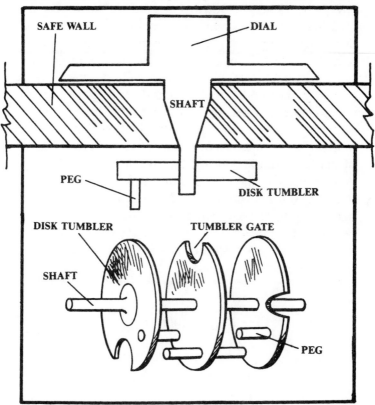

Figure 32. Here is a modern disk tumbler dial system (top), and a set of disk tumblers (above).

Disk tumbler locks work by the use of flat, round disks of metal or plastic with a notch and a peg on each disk. The notch is called the tumbler gate. The gate of each tumbler has to be lined up with the pawl of the bolt mechanism by usage of the linking capabilities of the pegs.

The first tumbler of the disk tumbler lock (also the last combination number dialed) is mechanically connected to the dial through the safe door. When the dial is turned, the first tumbler picks up the middle tumbler when their pegs connect. The middle tumbler in turn picks up the last tumbler for one more complete turn and the tumblers have been "cleared"—you are ready to dial the first combination number by aligning the last tumbler s gate to the pawl. After you have reached this number or position, rotate the dial in the opposite direction one complete turn (for three tumbler locks; two turns for four tumbler locks) to engage the middle tumbler and drive it to the second combination number. By rotating the dial back into the opposite direction to the last combination number, the bolt can be operated to open the lock, or as in the case of newer safes, the dial will operate the bolt by turning it once again in the opposite direction.

One of the innovations that developed to deter sensual manipulation of combination locks was the use of serrated front tumblers (last combination number dialed). These were designed to foil listening and feeling of the tumblers' gates by burglars.

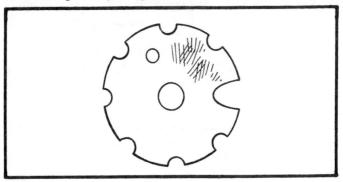

Figure 33. A serrated disk tumbler.

When the bolt encountered any one of these shallow gates, the safecracker could never be sure whether or not a tumbler was actually aligned with the pawl-bolt mechanism. Some burglars solved this problem by attaching high-speed drills to the dial knob to rotate and wear down the first tumbler's shallow false gates against the bolt, thereby eliminating them altogether, or at least minimizing their effects. Still, today the serrated tumbler is used as an effective deterrent to manipulation in combination padlocks where space is a factor.

Let us move on to combination padlocks. The most common and difficult to open of these small disk tumbler locks are the Master combination padlocks, and they are· quite popular. I have had good luck in opening these locks

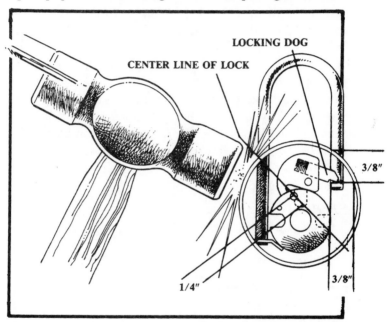

Figure 34. The simplest technique for opening combination locks.

with a wooden mallet or soft-faced hammer. The manipulation of Master combination padlocks is quite easy—I have done it thousands of times, and you can learn it, too. The newer the lock is, though, the more difficult it will be to open at first. If the lock has had a lot of use, such as that on a locker-room door where the shackle gets pulled down and encounters the tumblers while the combination is being dialed, the serrated front tumblers will become smoothed down, allowing easier sensing of the tumblers. So, until you have become good at opening these locks, practice extensively on an old one. Let's try to open one:

OPENING A COMBINATION PADLOCK

STEP ONE

First, clear the tumblers by engaging all of them. This is done by turning the dial clockwise (sometimes these locks open more easily starting in the opposite direction) three to four times. Now bring your ear close to the lock and gently press the bottom back edge to the bony area just forward of your ear canal opening so that vibrations can be heard and felt. Slowly turn the dial in the opposite direction. As you turn, you will hear a very light click as each tumbler is picked up by the previous tumbler. This is the sound of the pickup pegs on each disk as they engage each other. Clear the tumblers again in a clockwise manner and proceed to step two.

STEP TWO

After you have cleared the tumblers, apply an upward

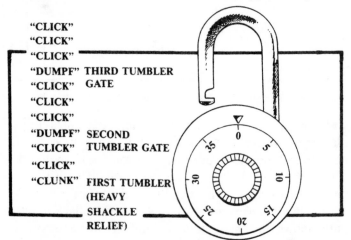

Figure 35. Listen carefully for the real gates when opening the combination padlock.

pressure on the shackle of the padlock. Keeping your ear on the lock, try to hear the tumblers as they rub across the pawl; keep the dial rotating in a clockwise direction.

You will hear two types of clicks, each with a subtle difference in pitch. The shallow, higher pitched clicks are the sound of the false gates on the first disk tumbler. Do not let them fool you—the real gates sound hollow and empty, almost nonexistent.

When you feel a greater than normal relief in the shackle once every full turn, this is the gate of the first tumbler (last number dialed). This tumbler is connected directly to the dial as mentioned earlier. Ignore that sound for now. When you have aligned the other two tumblers, the last tumbler's sound will be drowned out by the sound of the shackle popping open.

STEP THREE

While continuing in a clockwise direction with the dial, listen carefully for the slight hollow sound of either one of the first two tumblers. Note on the dial face where these sounds are by either memorizing them or writing them down. Make certain that you do not take note of the driv-

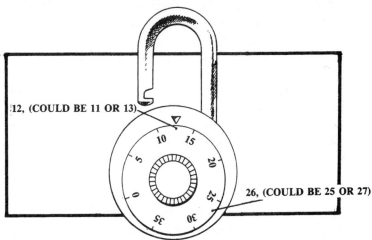

Figure 36. The hardest part of picking the combination padlock is done.

ing tumbler (last number dialed). If you hear and feel only one hollow click (sounds like "dumpf"), chances are that the first number could be the same as the last one.

You should have two numbers now. Let us say one of them is 12 and the other is 26. Clear the tumblers again just to be safe and stop at the number 12. Go counterclockwise one complete turn from 12. Continue until there is another "dumpf" sound. After the complete turn pass 12, if you feel and hear a louder than normal sound of a tumbler rubbing on the pawl, the first tumbler is properly aligned and the second tumbler is taking the brunt of the force from the shackle—you are on the right track. When the second tumbler has aligned in this case, you will feel a definite resistance with the last turn of the dial going clockwise. The final turn will automatically open the shackle of the lock. If none of these symptoms are evident, try starting with the number of the combination, 26, in the same way.

STEP FOUR

If the lock still does not open, don't give up. Try searching for a different first number. Give it a good thirty- or forty-minute try. If you play with it long enough, it will eventually open. The more practice you have under your belt, the quicker you will be able to open these padlocks in the future.

Using a stethoscope to increase audibility of the clicks is not out of the question when working on disk tumbler locks, though I never use them for padlocks. A miniature wide-audio-range electronic stethoscope with a magnetic base for coupling a piezoelectric-type microphone is ideal for getting to know the tumblers better.

Filing your fingertips to increase sensitivity might not be such a good idea for beginners since their fingertips will not be accustomed to operating dials for a long period of time. With practice, you may develop calluses and need to file your fingertips. But I don't recommend it at first.

After some time you may find that in some cases you can whiz right through the combination of an unknown lock without looking at it and pop it open in seconds. It becomes second nature. I've done this on many occasions—something beyond my conscious control seems to line up the tumblers without my thinking about it.

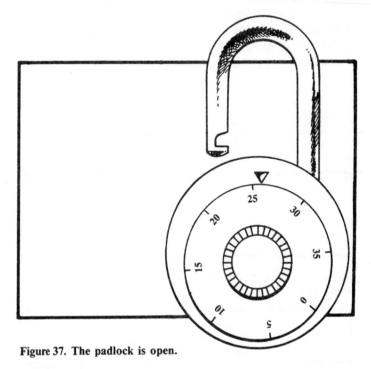

Figure 37. The padlock is open.

Another type of disk tumbler padlock is the Sesame lock made by the Corbin Lock Co. Its unique design makes it more difficult to open than Master padlocks, but it can be opened. Let's take one of the three or four wheel mechanisms, look at a cross section, and see how it works. The wheel has numbers from zero to nine. Attached to the wheel is a small cam. Both the wheel and cam turn on the shaft. Each wheel in this lock operates independently with its own cam and shaft. The locking dog is locked to the shackle. In this position the shackle cannot be opened. The locking dog operates with all three or four wheels. The locking dog is riding on the round edge of the cam. The spring is pushing up on the cam. The locking dog cannot move up because it is resting on the round part of the cam. When the wheel is turned to the proper combination number, the locking dog rests on the flat of the cam. The spring can then raise the locking dog to release the shackle, and this opens the lock.

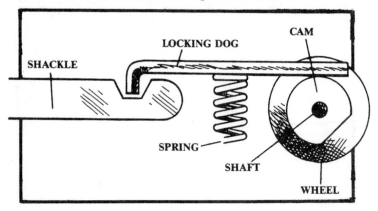

Figure 38. The Corbin Sesame padlock has a complicated opening mechanism.

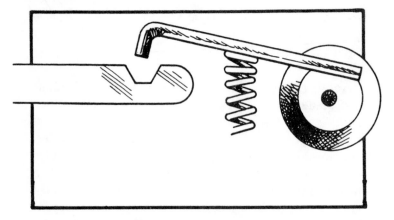

Figure 39. But the Sesame padlock can be manipulated open.

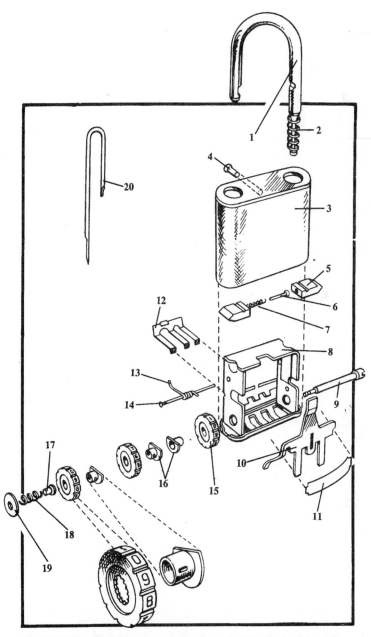

Figure 40. The Corbin Sesame padlock. 1: shackle; 2: shackle spring; 3: case; 4: rivet; 5: bolts; 6: alignment pin; 7: bolt spring; 8: housing; 9: wheel shaft; 10: dog plate; 11: anti-vibrator spring; 12: stop lever plate; 13: spring for dog plate; 14: spring pivot pin; 15: wheels; 16: slide bearing (cams); 17: bearing; 18: pressure; 19: lock nut for wheel shaft; 20: change pin.

Tips for Success

You will undoubtedly encounter a pin tumbler lock in which there will be a pin or two that is keyed too low (the shear line of the pin is too high). In this case the lock is difficult to open because the breaking point of a long bottom pin doesn't allow room in the keyway for the pick to manipulate the other pins. Your success in opening "tight" locks will depend on the skill you have developed with your tension wrench. Sometimes it helps to play with the tension wrench. Try bouncing it left and right slightly while picking, allowing some of the tumblers to drop occasionally. You may also try picking the front tumblers first or picking at random on these locks. You can tell if you have a lock that is keyed like this because your pick may get jammed during the picking process.

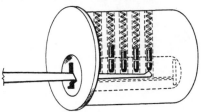

Figure 41. Some pin tumbler locks are tricky to pick.

After you have opened a cylinder and unlocked a lock, be sure to return it to the locked position. You will hear the tumblers click into place when this happens. Otherwise it may be difficult to unlock it with its key because the bottom pins cannot "float" like they normally would.

To tell whether or not the cylinder should go clockwise or counterclockwise when picking a tumbler lock, there is an easy rule to follow. If the tumblers (pin or wafer) will not break, or stay broken, you are going in the wrong direction with the tension wrench. There will be little or no progress with the cylinder, and few, if any, "clicks."

Some keyways are cut at an angle (Yale, Dexter, and Schlage, for example) so you want to be sure that you tilt your pick to follow that angle while picking or your pick will get hung up. A slight twist of the wrist will compensate for this problem.

Should your fingers become tired while picking a lock, lay down your tools and shake your hands and fingers to relieve any tension. After some time the muscles in your hands will become accustomed to such activity. Practice and persistence will tone your hands and senses to the point where you will be able to pop open a cylinder in three to five seconds (that's *seconds*) in total darkness. The combination of touch and sound lets you know almost a split second before you open the lock that you have succeeded.

If the lock is a well-machined one, the cylinder will feel

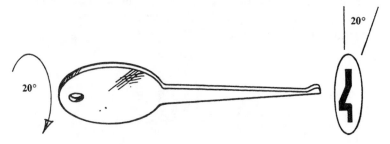

Figure 42. Some locks require that the pick be inserted at a slight angle.

tight and you will need a little firmer hand on the tension wrench. While picking, if any one of the pins at any time feels firm or difficult to move, chances are it's aligned. If it feels springy, it is not.

Use the shaft of the pick if you have to when working the frontal pin of a pin tumbler lock. This may save you the trouble of aligning the tip of the pick on the front pin where there is little or no support for the pick. All of the other pins allow the pick to be supported by the inside wall of the keyway.

Master keyed pin tumbler locks are generally easier to pick open because they have more than one shear line or breaking point in the pins. Master keying allows a group of locks to be controlled by a master key holder while the individual locks in that group are controlled by individual keys. Hotels and apartment complexes are usually master keyed.

There is a simple technique to open pin and wafer tumbler locks. Simply drill through the shear lines of the tumblers. This point is located just above the center of the keyway on the face of the cylinder. By doing this, though, you obviously ruin the lock and make a lot of racket. If the lock is a Medeco or some other high-security lock, you risk damage of one hundred dollars or more, so be sure you know the value of the situation before you decide to rape the lock. Use a center punch to start a reliable hole on the cylinder face and use a one-quarter inch drill bit with a variable speed drill. With a large screwdriver, turn it to unlock. The cylinder will be difficult to turn because you may be shearing the tumbler springs that have fallen down past the cylinder's shear line.

Dead bolt locks are those mounted on a door above the knob. All dead bolt locks unlock counterclockwise with left-hand doors and clockwise with righthand doors. If you have trouble remembering this, just remember that the bolt of the lock has to go in the opposite direction of the doorjam.

Dead bolt locks are just as easy to pick open as knob locks are. They both have cylinders that can be picked open. The main difference is that dead bolts cannot be opened by sliding a plastic or metal card through to the bolt so as to work it back. In other words, they are not spring loaded. That's why they are called *dead* bolts. Most knob locks now have guards in front of the bolts to deter opening with cards.

Kwik-sets, Weisers, and some of the less-expensive knob locks may open in either direction. Schlage and Corbin, along with more sophisticated locks, can open only in one direction. Auto locks will open either way. Another method of picking pin tumbler locks is with a pick gun. As the pick snaps up, it hits the bottom pin. This bounces the top pin out of the cylinder and into the shell. As you apply light turning pressure with the tension wrench, the top pins are caught in the shell, the cylinder will turn. I've never used a pick gun, but they do work well for locksmiths who use them. They are cumbersome and expensive, and show some lack of professionalism.

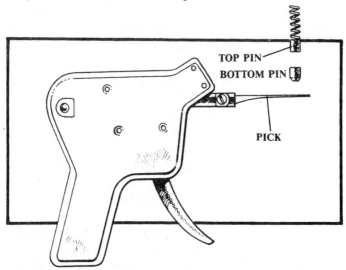

TOP PIN

BOTTOM PIN

PICK

Figure 43. Pick guns are for those who can't take the time to learn the fine art of lock picking.

SOME PRECAUTIONS

If you bought this book to learn how to pick locks in order to become a more efficient burglar, then there is not a whole lot I can say or do to stop you. But I must say this: the locks used in prisons are nearly impossible to pick even if you get or make the right tools. They are usually electrically controlled from an external station. Do not carry lock picks on your person. If you get caught with them, you could get nailed for most any professional job in town for the last seven years. If you must carry them, as in the case of rescue workers, etc., please consult your local authorities about details and ask about registering with them. As a former locksmith, I do not have that problem.

I advise that you do not teach your friends how to pick locks. The choice is yours, of course. You paid the price of this book and the knowledge is yours—be selfish with it. It is for your own protection as well. The fewer people who know you have this skill, the better. Getting blamed for something you didn't do is unfair and a hassle.

When you become proficient at picking locks, you may decide to get a job as a locksmith. But believe me, there is more to being a locksmith than being able to pick locks. You have to be a good carpenter as well as a fair mechanic. But you may want to approach the owner of a lock shop and ask if you could get on as an apprentice.

NOBODY'S PERFECT

There isn't a locking device on earth that cannot be opened with means other than its key or code. It's just that some are easier to open than others. Anything with a keyhole, dial, or access port is subject to being opened with alternate means, though some of the newer electronic and computer-controlled security devices would be a nightmare even if you had extensive knowledge of electronics and electromagnetics. Some devices also use palm prints as a readout to allow entry.

On the mechanical side, there are locks that have normal pin tumblers, but they are situated in various places 360 degrees around the cylinder. Some locks use pin tumblers that not only have to be aligned vertically within the cylinder, but also have to "twist" or turn a certain number of degrees to allow the cylinder to open. This is because the pins' shear line is cut at an angle. These locks are made by Medeco.

I have witnessed only one Medeco lock being picked— by a fellow locksmith. We both spent hours trying to pick it again, but it was futile. We estimated the chances of opening it again to be one out of 10,000. They are excellent security devices, but their price keeps them limited to areas prone to security problems such as isolated vending machines and for government use. The only one I have been successful at opening (after an hour of picking) was one I drilled. By the way, they are easy to drill because the brass that's used is soft.

LEARNING TO TOUCH AND FEEL

Most of us know how to touch. We touch objects every day, and yet we do not truly feel them. It seems so commonplace that we forget that we are actually feeling while we touch.

Here is an exercise that will develop a delicate touch. Gently rub and massage your hands and fingers— preferably with hand lotion. Do this for five minutes. Once the lotion has evaporated, shake your hands and fingers so that they flop loosely. Gently pull each finger to relax each joint.

Now with a piece of fine sandpaper, gently draw the tips of your fingers across it. Try to feel the texture of the grains on its surface. Relax your fingers, hands, forearms, shoulders, and chest. Take your time. Do this for several minutes.

After a few weeks of practice, you will be able to feel each individual grain of sand on the sandpaper. This allows you to feel the slightest sensation vibrate through your bones.

Try to remember to practice touching and feeling during your everyday experiences. Practice feeling wood, metal, and various other objects. Play with the feel of mechanical vibrations, even your television set. Try to sense the world around you as a source of information. This could and will open a whole new horizon of experience.

After a while, you will be able to feel or sense the movement of the tumblers of a Sargeant and Greenleaf safe. My first safe opened in three minutes because of that technique that took me years to discover.

VISUALIZATION

If you respect the security of the lock and do not become overconfident, you will never become disappointed if you fail to open it. You also increase your chances of opening the lock because you personally have nothing to gain or lose by opening it. Give up trying to be an expert and just pick the lock.

With such an attitude, you may find the lock will usually pop right open. I never received a trophy for being the best lock picker in the state. My satisfaction is in knowing that I am never helpless in a lockout situation. The quality of your success is almost romantic; it involves sensitivity and compassion in the face of curiosity as a means to help others.

Visualization and imagination are important to the lock picker. I've noticed that people who have the ability to visualize the internal parts of the lock that they are picking seldom fail to open it in moments. Anyone can learn to do this by simply remembering to do it while picking a lock. Since sight, sound, and touch are involved with the process, visualization is very easy to do. Try to keep all of your attention on the lock during the picking process. This will help you to learn how to use heightened sensitivity for picking locks.

So in that respect, an unopened lock is like a new and unexplored lover. You imagine all of the qualities of an attractive person whom you've just met and apply that feeling to the lock that you are picking. Use visualization. It will help immensely.